AF594212

From
Football to Finance
THE STORY OF BRADY KEYS, JR.

BY ERIC B. ROBERTS

From Football to Finance

THE STORY OF BRADY KEYS, JR.

HBJ Harcourt Brace Jovanovich, Inc., New York

Curriculum-Related Books are relevant to current interests of young people and to topics in the school curriculum.

First Edition

ISBN 0-15-230265-4

Library of Congress Catalog Card Number: 70–151026

Printed in the United States of America

CREDITS FOR ILLUSTRATIONS

All-Pro Enterprises, Inc.: p. 83; Anderson High School: p. 15; Lin Caufield Photographers Inc.—Louisville, Kentucky: p. 87; Colorado State University Photograph: p. 19; Claude Desautels: p. 91; East Los Angeles Jr. College: p. 17; First National City Bank: p. 60; Raoul Gradvohl: p. 9; Photo by Harris in the *New Pittsburgh Courier*: pp. 22–23; Harry Homa: p. 27; Brady Keys, Jr.: p. 43; Aaron Latham, *The Washington Post,* September 16, 1970, © *The Washington Post:* p. 90; Copyright, 1967, *Los Angeles Times,* reprinted by permission: p. 36; *Nation's Restaurant News:* p. 85; Palmer Studio: p. 98; Pittsburgh Steelers: pp. 33, 35; Polytechnic High School: p. 15; Paul Russell Photography: pp. 53, 55, 72; St. Louis Football Cardinals: p. 67; Irv Schankman—Dorrill St. Louis: p. 64.

Table of Contents

From
Football to Finance
THE STORY OF BRADY KEYS, JR.

Preface

This is the era of the non-person, the anti-hero and the disenchantment of youth.

It is an era when Horatio Alger plots are as out-of-date as leather headgears.

Brady Keys grew up in this point in time and his early accomplishments give him extraordinary credentials for the future.

He spent his early years in Austin, Texas. He was poor and, as he puts it, "appeared to be just another one of the countless, nondescript black boys—doomed to a lifetime of emptiness, inside some ghetto."

After high school, he wandered aimlessly from job to job before joining the Eagle Rock semi-pro football team in Los Angeles. At the time, Keys apparently considered this a simple diversion in his purposeless life. Actually it provided the spark that sent him reaching for the moon.

His semi-pro play was so outstanding, especially in a scrimmage against the Los Angeles Rams, that scouts at that game convinced this young man that there was some worth in all the old assumptions and moralities.

He selected Colorado State as his school. But when he enrolled he was a few years older and wiser than his classmates. He made his mark both scholastically and athletically.

It is at this point in his life that I can speak with most knowledge. He played for the Pittsburgh Steelers. I am the owner of that team.

He gave us every ounce of his ability on the playing field and he was fair and realistic in his negotiations off the field. Perhaps his rag-tag early days gave him a better sense of values than most.

A great example of his playing ability came in 1963. Keys was a cornerback on the defensive unit. A great many experts believe this is the most difficult defensive position in football. And when you make a mistake, you make it out in the open before God and usually some 50,000 fans.

In 1963, not one of the exceptional wide receivers in the National Football League caught a touchdown pass on Brady. Neither sports writers nor the fans keep any statistics on that kind of feat, but it is an exceptional statistic, especially in those pass-conscious days of the long bomb.

He used both confidence and ingenuity to psyche his enemies on the playing field. He attempted to take away their concentration by talking to them. It worked with a lot of folks, Keys once said, but never with Raymond Berry. Berry was the great Baltimore end that teamed up with Johnny Unitas to make life impossible for Brady Keys.

Today Brady Keys has become a successful businessman, a recognized leader not only in the black community but in the community PERIOD.

To help him along the way, Keys refers to the philosophy of William DuBois, a famed black intellectual and the patron saint of some of the more militant societies. Go into business, urged DuBois, in order to develop the wealth and power needed to change the black man's position in American society.

Brady Keys is trying.

ART ROONEY

November 27, 1970

1

A Running Start

On a Friday afternoon, in the black ghetto of East Austin, Texas, Coach Jack Crawford watched his Kealing Junior High School varsity football unit assemble for the 1950 season's first scrimmage.

Two weeks of intensive training, including daily five-mile jogs, had prepared every player for action. Even the smaller, younger members of the B-team unit, certain to take a beating from the varsity, were filled with ambition as they lined up to receive the kickoff.

The referee blew his whistle. Shoe leather sounded against the teed-up ball, and twenty-two keyed-up players sped toward contact. The ball soared 55 yards and settled in the arms of the B-team's Brady

Keys, Jr. Brady took off. He evaded two varsity defenders at his own 35-yard line, then sprang free of the others with a burst of speed at midfield.

While Coach Crawford looked on in disbelief, a pair of varsity mates closed in on Brady at the varsity 25. Shifting the ball to his left hand, Brady's stiff-arm caught one pursuer off balance and flattened him at the 16-yard line. But Brady was unable to regain top speed before the other man overtook him and cut him down at the varsity 9.

In a rage, Coach Crawford grabbed a long paddle and shouted at the varsity to line up at midfield.

"You no-tackling babies—you spineless jackasses!" he roared. "You let a thirteen-year-old child run through you, the length of the field, like a jackrabbit! I'm going to use this paddle on your tails. I'm taking it out on your hides."

Billy Owens, 190-pound, six-foot varsity captain, protested. "Coach, that Keys kid has a reputation for being fast and tricky. We made the mistake of letting him get. . . ."

"Shut up!" roared the coach. "Shut up, and take it on the tail!"

Every victim groaned and, under his breath, cursed both the coach and Keys.

"We'll get the little rascal if he carries the ball again," the captain vowed. "The little punk thinks he's really tough. We've got to show him who's boss."

Yet the varsity defense was less confident than before, as it lined up for a second kickoff to the B-team.

All eyes followed Brady as he moved to the B-team's 5-yard line. The ball was kicked. Brady moved forward and received it at his 10-yard line as the varsity came barreling downfield. Seeing that the charge was loaded to the outside, left and right, Brady took off up the middle. Leaping over flattened blockers and felled defenders, he tore through a tangle of tacklers and was free again at midfield.

At the varsity 45, Brady tricked one player, wrenched free of a second, and was trying to evade a third when he was grabbed from behind by Captain Owens. Hit from both sides, Brady disappeared under the deadweight of two vicious varsity tacklers.

Badly shaken, Brady lay still for several seconds. As varsity members grinned with pleasure, he got up and walked unsteadily to the B-team bench.

Coach Crawford came over to look at him. "Are you all right, Brady?" Brady lifted his head. "They really hit me, Coach, but that's all right. I like to hit hard, too. I can take it."

Coach Crawford studied Brady. "Go home, son," the coach said. "Get a warm bath and take it easy. You'll be okay. Be back out here tomorrow for signals and wind sprints."

As Brady walked outside, he could hear Coach Crawford's scolding voice. "That green kid made all of you supposed varsity look helpless. If he can run 91 and 65 yards against you, we've got a long way to go."

As Brady walked towards his home on East 21st Street, two miles away, he felt pain in the area around his right hip. But there was a smile on his face as he remembered what else Coach Crawford had said to the varsity: "If Owens hadn't been lucky enough to grab Brady from behind, that thirteen-year-old kid would have rolled 90 yards to the goal line."

He thought of something else Coach Crawford had said: "Too bad he won't get a chance to play for the University of Texas Longhorns when he grows up."

As he strode along, Brady flexed his arms and pounded his hard, flat stomach. "I'm in good shape," he thought. "I can take the poundings." The words rolled off his tongue: "I'm ready—really ready."

The confident words, however, did not completely convince Brady. He was worried. Dr. Washington, the school athletic physician, had told Brady that he had a bad heart.

Brady refused to let himself believe Dr. Washington's diagnosis. For years, without incident, he had taken part in different sports. Now, if the doctor were right, Brady would be through with sports. And Brady believed that he had no future without football. So, although he knew he was cheating, Brady decided that Dr. Washington had made a mistake, and he altered the doctor's report before handing it in to the athletic office.

"You're home early," his mother said, smiling at him from the porch. Putting aside his troublesome thoughts, Brady recounted the afternoon's events for her.

Brady Keys' mother.

Brady's mother, A. C., had devoted her life to raising her son properly. Divorced when Brady was very young, she had worked hard to support them, and Brady learned quickly how to be his own man, to help out by doing odd jobs, like washing dishes in the mess hall at the University of Texas, where All-American Bobby Layne was having a sensational Longhorn career. Layne, gifted on offense, was one of Brady's heroes.

Brady's mother had received help from the Wheeler family, for whom she was working as a domestic when Brady was born. It seemed to her that Brady led an integrated life from the beginning because the Wheelers treated her and Brady like members of their own family. Brady was sick when he was a baby and the Wheelers made sure that he got the proper food and specialists to get well.

The Wheelers also encouraged Brady's mother to train herself for a profession that she would enjoy. She decided to attend beauty school.

She had no problems with Brady.

When Brady was nine, A. C. remarried. She hoped that her marriage to Garland Franklin would make a better life possible for Brady. Her new husband even planned to help her open a beauty parlor. Brady, however, had trouble adjusting to the marriage. He resented having to share his mother. And later, when his mother and stepfather decided to move to Los Angeles, he resented having to leave Austin.

At Kealing Junior High, Brady had moved up to

the varsity. Coach Crawford was impressed with him and predicted an exciting football career for him. Brady also had developed several deep friendships in school. He hated to leave.

So Brady was permitted to remain in Austin with his aunt, Mrs. Clara Daniels, until the end of the school year.

Inevitably, however, the day came for Brady to leave Austin. Aunt Clara and a buddy, Reggie Smith, accompanied Brady to the railroad station at sundown. His trunk was checked, his hand luggage lifted onto the reversed seat opposite him. Brady looked through the sealed window at Reggie and Aunt Clara. They both smiled, and his aunt threw him a last kiss. He felt the long train begin to move. The last thing Brady saw was Aunt Clara, Reggie, and several late-arrived friends waving good-bye under the "Colored" sign hung over a station doorway.

Sitting back in his seat, Brady found himself humming "California, here I come." He laughed at himself and settled down for the long journey.

2

The Road to Pittsburgh

The distance from Austin, Texas, to Los Angeles, California, is over 1,300 miles. On the Southern Pacific Railway in June, 1951, Brady Keys, Jr., spent a day and a half covering that distance.

After bidding his Aunt Clara and his pal Reggie good-bye at the station in Austin, Brady ate the fried chicken and French-fried potatoes that his aunt had packed in a shoe box for him. During the rest of the trip, he munched on some fruit and odd snacks he purchased on the train.

The ride was wearing, and soon became boring. The motion of the train lulled him into a half-sleeping state.

Los Angeles! The hugeness of the city startled Brady and thoroughly awakened him. He was so overwhelmed that he was hardly conscious of his mother's welcoming kiss and his stepfather's handshake. He was more aware of feeling an eagerness to do something in Los Angeles that would force that big city to notice that Brady Keys, Jr., was there.

Brady had always made friends easily, and in Los Angeles he soon became friends with a boy named Dale Everett, who lived in the same section of L.A., the Manual Arts area, as Brady. Dale, however, attended a different school, Polytechnic High. Brady wanted to be with his friend; so A. C. arranged a transfer to Polytechnic.

In high school, Brady became a four-sport sensation, but football was his true love. He first distinguished himself under Coach Voel Brenner and continued to excel under Coach Bob Beck.

A high point of that period was the 1953 game between Los Angeles High and Polytechnic, with Polytechnic a three-touchdown underdog. Battered and bruised, Brady was sidelined late in the third quarter, when Polytechnic was down, 20–18. With seconds left in the game, Brady returned to the field and, before a crowd of 20,000, zigzagged 65 yards to a 24–20 Polytechnic victory.

The following year, when Brady suffered a frightening injury that threatened to cripple him, the grateful Polytechnic student body raised the money to pay for a knee operation. The doctors' pessimistic

Brady as a freshman in high school.

In one of many spectacular plays, Brady carries the ball 65 yards for a touchdown against Belmont High School.

predictions of how long it would be before he would walk again, if ever, were a challenge to Brady. Eleven days after the operation, he was walking—insisting he was ready for football.

His success in meeting this challenge deepened Brady's confidence in his ability to overcome any obstacle. However, it also encouraged a tendency in Brady not to listen to advice, even when based on knowledge and experience superior to his own. This trait would involve him in trouble in the future.

As he neared the end of high school, he rejected a $10,000 Brooklyn Dodgers offer to play baseball, and contemplated the college offers.

Brady had scholarship offers from the University of California at Los Angeles (UCLA) and the University of Southern California (USC), as well as from colleges in other parts of the country. The USC people knew that Brady was going to be a tremendous football player. One of the coaches had already tagged him the equal of a contemporary All-American great at the University of Minnesota, Paul Giel. So they sent an alumnus, Walter D. Thomas, to persuade Brady to accept their offer. Thomas talked realistically with Brady about his future. He urged Brady to plan for the time when his football days would be over by preparing himself in college for a career in business. He showed him that stardom on a nationally noted team like the USC Trojans could be used as a stepping stone into the white-dominated business world.

Brady, however, was hard to sell. He refused to

At East Los Angeles Junior College, Brady (left) excelled in track as well as football.

go along with Thomas' advice and rejected USC's offer.

Although he was interested in accepting the scholarship offer from UCLA, Brady could not get himself interested in going to school to study. His grades were bad. However, he was impressed with UCLA Coach Red Sanders. So he enrolled at East Los Angeles Junior College to try and bring his grades up and make up a credit he lacked, in order to meet UCLA's entrance requirements.

Brady's attempt to gain college-entrance status at East Los Angeles was brief. Unable to organize himself and his school work, Brady dropped out after a year.

For a while, Brady drifted. Free of the demands of athletic training, he partied with a vengeance, while working at unskilled, low-paying jobs.

Brady could not stay away from football very long, however, so he joined the Eagle Rock Athletic Club, a semi-professional unit. Brady was unhappy at first because he was playing behind ex-All-Americans Aramis Dandoy and Addison Hawthorne, former USC starters. When he was moved up to be the key back—ahead of both Dandoy and Hawthorne—Brady was encouraged. He thought about going to Canada the next season and starring in the Canadian Football League.

While Brady was thinking about Canada, the Los Angeles Rams arranged a three-team doubleheader at the Rose Bowl as the lid-lifter for the 1958 season. During the first half, the Rams played the Eagle Rock eleven; during the second, another team.

Brady was superb. He carried ten times for more than 100 yards. His six-foot, 172-pound frame created a continual headache for the pros. One of the scouts at the game, Fido Murphy of the Pittsburgh Steelers, asked Brady to sign with the Steelers as a member of the taxi squad. Brady felt insulted by the offer and rejected it.

Murphy's second suggestion was the right idea at the right time. He offered Brady the chance to go to college at Colorado State University until he could be legally drafted as a free agent.

Brady was interested. He was 21-years-old, and he thought he was ready to settle down. He had fallen in love with Anna Marie Woodson, and they married before setting out for Colorado State University at Fort Collins, 1,160 miles away.

Brady starred for Colorado State University.

The first year was tough going in more ways than one. The young couple found that living on a scholarship could sometimes mean going hungry, so Brady went hunting and fishing to provide more food. And even though this cut into study time, he maintained a 3.2 grade average.

With the steadying influence of his wife and an additional monthly allowance, Brady was able to settle down his second year at Colorado. He played impressive ball, and the Pittsburgh Steelers were now able to draft him for the next season.

3

Rookie Steeler

In 1946, Paul Brown, the coach of the trailblazing Cleveland Browns, had brought blacks back into professional football, but black rookies did not appear with the Pittsburgh Steelers until 1961. That summer, Coach Buddy Parker invited nine black rookies to try out for positions that would guarantee good salaries.

There was excitement in the air as the veteran players eyed and rated the nine rookies. Only five black Steelers, all National Football League veterans, were there: Fullback John Henry Johnson, Offensive Guard John Nisby, Offensive End Fred Williamson, and two acquisitions from the Baltimore Colts—Eugene "Big Daddy" Lipscomb, at tackle, and Cornerback John Sample. (Jack McClairen had retired to a head football coach spot, and Willie McClung, offensive lineman, had been dealt to the Detroit Lions.)

The big question that day was how many of the black rookies would be retained. Everyone's attention was focused on the midfield, where Assistant Coach Mike Nixon was working with the rookies. Coach Parker watched Nixon as he tested 185-pound Brady Keys, Jr.

Parker, who had been a star halfback on the NFL championship-winning Detroit Lions of 1935, liked what he saw. Five days later, after six black rookies had been eliminated, Brady remained with the team. This Brady Keys would not miss. He had a single thought in his head—to drive somebody out of that starting Steelers' backfield.

Tom Tracy was the right-halfback of record. Two years before, the five-foot-ten, 210-pound Tracy had gained a total of 794 yards on 199 ball-carrying

In 1961, Keys, number 26, competed with eight other black rookies for positions with the Steelers.

attempts to become the Steelers' "Bomb." No other Steeler back had equaled him. (Although a former Steelers star, Byron "Whizzer" White, now a Justice of the Supreme Court, once led the NFL with 587 yards on 152 carries.) However, some of the other Steelers thought that Tom's best days were over.

Halfback Dick Hoak, a Penn State candidate, was another tough rival facing Brady. He prayed and waited for an opportunity to carry the ball and demonstrate his skill.

The Steelers and the Baltimore Colts opened their exhibition seasons that year in Roanoke, Virginia. Brady, to his delight, was a member of both the kicking and receiving teams on kickoffs. The Baltimore coaching staff, however, was aware of his reputation for field-length kickoff and punt returns and the Colts disappointed Brady by deliberately kicking to Bill Butler, a three-year Steeler veteran.

Three times the Colts kicked to Butler, while Brady led the downfield charge as Butler's blocker. On one run, Brady even flattened six-foot-six, 272-pound Sherman Plunkett of the Colts' defensive unit, but he wanted to dazzle the Colts with a 100-yard scamper. Frustrated and angry, Brady decided that Butler was hogging the kickoffs. The more he thought about it, the angrier he became, until he was in a rage. He jumped up from the bench where he and Butler were sitting and, grabbing the veteran, challenged him to "have it out."

Two veteran Steelers, one white and one black, grabbed and restrained Brady, who was yelling at

Butler that he should give him one of the kickoffs.

Since neither player was injured, Coach Parker was tolerant. "Don't worry, boy," Parker said. "You're going to have plenty of opportunities to show what you can do for this ball club."

At this point, when the tough world of professional football was making a place for him, Brady suffered another injury that threatened to end his career.

The place was Forbes Field, Pittsburgh. The occasion was the Detroit Lions against the Steelers in their second exhibition game. Brady felt good as he accepted the opening kickoff at the Steelers' 10 and started running along the eastern sideline. At the Steelers 35, hurdling a mass of mixed jersies, Brady fell forward onto his back. Lucius Jackson, the Lions' lineman, stumbled onto Brady's face, collapsing his inadequate, single-ribbed protector that was popular then. A cleat pushed Brady's right eye back into his head and fractured his nose.

Bleeding badly from both nostrils and groaning with pain, Brady staggered around, crying: "I can't see! I can't see!" It seemed to be the end of football for Brady.

After a couple of days had passed to allow the swelling to subside, Brady again underwent a delicate operation. Two weeks later, the operation was deemed a success, and once again Brady had overcome a tremendous obstacle.

Brady was confident that he would make the starting offensive eleven in 1961. He worked hard the very least, he believed that he had justified the Steelers' advance of a $1500 bonus, most of which he and Anna used up getting to Pittsburgh. He also was sure he was earning the $8,000-a-year salary that gave him and Anna a feeling of security. He felt ready for the season to begin.

September 16 was the opening game against the New York Giants. Parker named as the starting backfield Johnson, Tracy, Bobby Layne, and Flanker Buddy Dial. Of the nine black rookies who had reported in late July, only Brady and Len Burnett remained. Brady was to be back-up man for Tracy. Burnett was slated to play as right cornerback—teamed up with John Sample.

A crowd of 38,000 fans gathered at Pitt Stadium for the game. During the second quarter of the evenly contested game, Coach Parker decided to have a look at Keys in the running back slot beside Johnson at fullback.

Signaled to run a strong-side, off-tackle weave, Brady took the handoff from Layne, then noticed that the left-side members of the Giants' defensive frontal (Tackle Dick Modzelowski and End Jim Katcavage) had shed the Steeler blockers and were crossing the scrimmage line.

Certain he would get nothing on their side, Brady reversed his field, tore himself free of Jim Robustelli, the Giants' right end, and angled outside for a 22-yard pickup. It was first down for Pittsburgh at New York's 46-yard line.

During his first season with the Steelers, Keys proved his ability as a first-string defensive half-back.

26

Proud of his first-down carry, Brady started back to the Steelers' huddle. He was startled when Tracy tapped him to take his position in the huddle. Confused, Brady went back to the bench and Coach Parker.

Parker was furious. "Boy, you'll never run another offensive play on this team as long as I'm the coach," he said. "Get one thing straight: nobody runs a reverse-field option on me."

Terrible words. At first, they overwhelmed Brady. He wondered if he was finished as a Steeler before getting started. Then he calmed himself, reasoning that Parker had spoken in anger and would also calm down. What a reaction to his first pro effort!

A week later, Brady was back at work. Burnett injured his leg and Parker moved Brady into Len's cornerback spot.

Keys and Sample made a brilliant brace of cornerbacks. Both were great open field runners with good footwork and blazing speed. Both were dangerous on punt returns, and both could carry interceptions the length of a gridiron across enemy goal lines.

Brady took Sample as his model and took to heart all his advice. "Talk tough," Sample warned. "Hard hitting and loud talking will force the pros to respect you."

4

The Making of a Pro

In December 1962, when Art Rooney, Sr., president of the Pittsburgh Steelers, flew with the team to Washington, D.C., for the final game of the season, few professional outfits had better prospects than the Steelers.

Nobody was more aware of that fact than Head Coach Buddy Parker. In 1958, he had resigned his position as head coach of the Detroit Lions, then the champions of the National Football League. It had taken him five years to forge the long-downtrodden Steelers into a contender with a 9–5 win-loss record in 1962, the only Steelers team to win that many games in 37 seasons of NFL play.

Since November, his Steelers had become difficult

opponents. At Philadelphia, the Eagles lost 27–16. At Yankee Stadium, the Giants lost 20–17. The St. Louis Cardinals were trounced 19–7 at Pittsburgh, where the Steelers also triumphed 23–21, over the Washington Redskins, with a last-minute rally.

Parker knew he had constructed a bone crusher and he was planning on capturing Eastern Division honors in 1963. He had a four-man defensive frontal that would make it almost impossible to run against the Steelers of 1963: John Baker, six-foot-six, 282 pounds, at left end; Joe Krupa, six-foot-three, 256 pounds, left tackle; Big Daddy Lipscomb, six-foot-seven, 292 pounds, right tackle; Ernie Stautner, six-foot-three, 227 pounds, right end.

The Steelers beat the Redskins, and, although they then lost to Detroit in the Playoff Bowl, Coach Parker continued to look forward to 1963.

Two weeks after the defeat, Lipscomb's outstanding performance in the Pro Bowl made the outlook for the '63 season even more promising. Lipscomb was so good that, when he left the game in the last quarter, the crowd stood and cheered.

In May 1963, the Steelers were stunned by the tragic news of Lipscomb's death. The Steelers seemed to be jinxed, as they arrived at Pitt Stadium in September for the opening game of the '63 season against the Giants. They came away from that game with renewed confidence after trouncing New York, 31–0. Baker and Brady were especially aggressive that day, with Brady successfully putting into effect John Sample's advice.

After New York, the Steelers defeated the Dallas Cowboys, 38–27. Then Parker's men met and conquered the St. Louis Cardinals, 23–10. In that game, however, the Steelers' jinx struck again, as John Henry Johnson badly sprained his ankle. Johnson had established a Steeler record of 1,151 net yards on 251 attempts in 1962. No team could lose a Lipscomb and a JHJ in a single season and keep the winning habit. Johnson missed the next five games.

At Philadelphia, the Steelers tied, 21–21. At St. Louis, they lost, 34–24, followed by a 35–25 defeat at Cleveland. The Steelers' undefeated four-game record became 4–3–2 before Johnson returned in November against the Cleveland Browns.

"With John Henry ready," predicted Brady, "we'll beat the Browns like breaking sticks." He was right. But the win was not without a price.

Realizing that Jim Brown, the six-two, 228-pound Cleveland fullback was their main problem, Brady and Clendenon Thomas—six-two, 200-pound free safety from the University of Oklahoma—had decided that the best way to handle Cleveland would be to tear into Brown on every play.

Their plan ran into difficulty late in the third quarter at Cleveland's 43-yard line. Keys had noted that Brown telegraphed his moves by glancing at the intended area of attack just before the snap of the ball. Thus, when the Browns came out of the huddle and Frank Ryan began sounding signals, Brady warned his middle linebacker: "Watch Brown, right up the middle."

Ryan handed off to Brown on an option thrust, inside or outside of Leo Cordileone's right tackle spot. Behind sharp blocking, Brown tore through the Steelers, past the middle linebacker, and into the open field.

Thomas charged forward, and Brady took aim at Brown from Pittsburgh's right side. Avoiding a head-on, Thomas developed toward his left for a side shot.

Brady had a clear shot at the Clevelander. Yet, at the last second, as Brady was about to throw a vicious elbow at Brown, Jim and Brady exchanged dagger glances. Switching from the elbow-throwing tactic, Brady jammed his shoulder against Brown's body, thereby exposing his rib cage to Brown's fist as Thomas ran headlong into the two of them at Pittsburgh's 31-yard line.

Trainers and water boys rushed onto the field from both benches. Thomas did not move, and was carried off the field. Keys and Brown got up painfully. Brady bled from the mouth, nose and both ears. Brown went over to his team mates. The doctors having stopped his bleeding, Brady, unaware that several of his ribs were fractured and a blood vessel ruptured, stayed in the game.

During the rest of the game, Brady kept on bleeding. That explosive play saved the day for Pittsburgh, but it meant the end of the 1963 season for Brady. In fact, Brady's injury was not properly identified and corrected until April 1964, five months later. Nonetheless, with Johnson back,

Brady heads for a pile-up with Jim Brown and Clendenon Thomas.

Coach Parker held onto his hopes for the Eastern Division title. The Dallas Cowboys were downed by the Steelers, 24–19. The Chicago Bears came to Pittsburgh on December 1 and left town with a 17–17 stalemate.

A week later, in Washington, D.C., the Steelers bested the Redskins, 34–28, to bring their record to 7–3–3 and .700.

In their final game against the Giants, whom they had wrecked, 31–0, in the opener, the Steelers saw the death of their hopes. They lost 33–17.

There were many excuses and explanations afterward. Nixon, the assistant coach, pointed out that Del Shofner, the New York Giant who contributed heavily to the Giants' victory, had been blanked by Brady in the opener. Nothing changed the fact, however, that the Eastern Division title did not belong to the Pittsburgh Steelers.

The following season, Coach Parker set up the training camp in Providence, Rhode Island. Because of his recent injury, Brady was scheduled for an intensive medical examination. At last, Brady had to face his old bugaboo, his heart condition.

When the doctor had finished checking his heart, Brady, dreading the answer, asked: "Doc, what's the final word?"

"Your heart's normal," the doctor informed him, dispelling, with a few simple words, the doubts Brady had harbored since the days of Keiling Junior High School.

During the next two seasons, Coach Parker, disappointed and frustrated by his team's failure to win the Eastern Division title, began dismissing his players. On the eve of the 1965 season, when Dan Rooney, the new executive vice president of the Steelers, intervened, Parker quit. During Brady's five years under Coach Parker, the Rooney team had posted a 26–20–2 record of wins-losses-ties. Brady, who had sharpened the John Sample method of intimidating ball carriers and pass catchers, could echo Sample's claim: "Not one touchdown pass has been completed in my territory this season."

In the early years, costly interference calls sometimes marred Brady's performance. In time, however, his methods became smoother. In 1966, NFL coaches paid tribute to his defensive finesse by picking him to start in the 1967 Pro Bowl.

The 1966 Steelers (Keys is front row, center).

JOHN HALL

The Keys Who Fits

When the Pro Bowlers make their annual scramble down the tunnel and out onto the Coliseum grass Sunday, it won't be too surprising if No. 26 of the East suddenly stops, looks around suspiciously and pinches himself.

"The Pro Bowl. It's been my biggest goal. It makes up for all the disappointments. I felt like I should have been here before, but now that I finally am it's like a dream. I wake up in the middle of the night and still can't believe it," said Brady Keyes of the Pittsburgh Steelers.

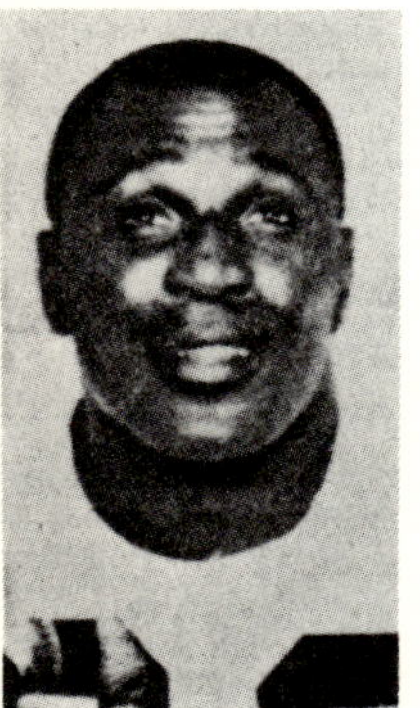

Brady Keys

Brady Keys? The name rings an old bell, but what's more obscure in these parts than a Steeler defensive back from Colorado State? The Steelers haven't even been out to visit the Rams since 1961.

Brady put it all together. "Yes," he said. "I'm the same Brady Keys who went to Poly High and was All-City in 1955."

His presence in the classic provides a hometown hero touch for a game almost totally lacking this time around in local-boy-makes-good dramatics.

Former Trojans Marlin McKeever and Willie Wood are on the West squad, but that's about it outside of little known No. 26.

Brady will open at right corner for Tom Landry's

The Los Angeles Times *paid tribute to Brady Keys when he returned to his home town for the 1967 Pro Bowl.*

The Pro Bowl was held at the Los Angeles Coliseum that year, sixteen years away from Kealing Junior High. As the names of the players were announced over the loudspeakers, drum rolls and the roar of the crowd accompanied each starter onto the field. Brady waited for his name.

"Brady Keys, Pittsburgh Steelers, right cornerback!" Head high, Brady sprinted into view. At that moment, nothing else existed for him besides that neat, green field.

That day, Brady faced Dave Parks, John Unitas, Gayle Sayers, and all the other greats of the West. And he and the East came away victorious, 27–14.

When the game was over, Brady felt a big letdown. He had met and matched the best. He had been a great runner, and he had switched to become equally skilled on defense. What football challenges were left? He had a good salary and was taking good care of his family. Where should he go next?

In the Pro Bowl, Keys races to intercept a pass intended for Gayle Sayers, number 40.

5

Franchise vs. Football

Following the victorious Pro Bowl, Brady and Anna celebrated with a family dinner. Brady's mother and stepfather and Anna's parents and her brother were there. Also present were six-year-old Brady Keys, 3d, and two-year-old Rodney, the baby of the Keys family.

An air of happiness and pride prevailed, as Anna and her mother began serving dinner. Brady at twenty-nine had a playing probability of at least six more seasons. He could earn at least $250,000 more before retiring.

"Well, folks," began Brady dramatically, "I'm afraid my football days are about done." All eyes were fixed on Brady as he continued. "I've reached every goal that I set for myself. I've proved I'm at least as good as the best. So now I've got to move toward something bigger and better."

Everyone became very quiet. Mrs. Cecile Bell, Anna's mother, finally said: "You mean you have something in mind that will pay as well as pro football, something you can keep on doing after you're thirty-six, right?" Brady smiled. "Cecile, you're dead right. I'm going into business. How do you like the chicken?" he asked, referring to the crisp, tasty main course. "Of course it's delicious," Brady replied to the appreciative comments. "That wonderful taste is the result of weeks of experimenting by A. C., Anna, Cecile and me to come up with a superb batter."

"We have so much confidence in our secret recipe that I plan to open the first Brady Keys' All-Pro Chicken store in San Diego two weeks from today."

Knowing Brady's determination when faced with a challenge, no one argued with his decision to try and build a business that he could fall back on when his football days were over.

While the announcement made it seem that Brady had made his decision suddenly, that was not the case. Brady's interest in business dated back to his last year at Polytechnic High when the idea was first planted in his mind by Walter Thomas. The University of Southern Califronia graduate, who had tried to persuade Brady to attend USC, had pointed out the advantages of a business career.

From the beginning of his great career with the

Pittsburgh Steelers, Brady thought about his future. He knew that a football career was a temporary experience. Thomas—who remained interested in him—and Brady debated for several years the importance of learning how the capitalistic system worked, and while he was in school at Colorado, Brady majored in business. And Brady improved the possibilities of future business success by becoming an outstanding football player.

As an employment interviewer at Douglas Aircraft between football seasons, Brady had been instrumental in placing quite a few blacks at Douglas. He had also worked with Jim Brown, in establishing his Black Economic Union. In both these experiences, Brady saw that there was a tremendous need for successful black businessmen so that black children would have someone other than sports figures to relate to. He believed that the continued success of this country rests in its youth, and in their involvement in the business mainstream of our country. Yet a young black, or even adult, who wanted to go into business just didn't have any models to follow. He felt business would be the perfect field in which to make a contribution to his people and an impact on the country.

Although Brady had never really heard the word "franchise," in the fall of 1966 he bought a book called *The Franchise Boom,* by Harry Kursh, and read it, to find out what franchising was all about. Both Brady and Jim Brown knew a man named Bill Stennis who was very successful in the chicken business, with a couple of "Golden Bird" stores in Los Angeles. Brady's first approach to going into business was to have Brown contact Bill Stennis and tell him that Brady wanted to make him a famous man by franchising his idea all over the country. Of course, Brady wanted a big piece of the action, and Bill refused him.

When the 1966 football season ended, Brady returned to Los Angeles and went to work in the restaurant of a friend, who had copied Stennis' operation, to learn the business. He worked in the store for nothing, taking his pay in experience. With funds borrowed from the Steelers because no bank would lend him money to go into business, and acting as his own contractor and interior designer, Brady was ready to open his own store.

Only Anna was briefed on his plans for securing the $5,000 he considered the amount needed to guarantee success for the first store. She knew, too, that her restless husband needed the challenge of building a coast-to-coast complex of franchises.

Two days later, Brady drove the 140-odd miles to San Diego. On Friday, January 27, at 4:30 P.M., Brady opened a store at 5067 Logan Street in San Diego. Certain that a determined man could accomplish anything, Brady envisioned long lines of customers waiting to eat All-Pro Fried Chicken.

The response that first day was encouraging: All-Pro Fried Chicken attracted $65 worth of business. "All I need," Brady decided, "are 200 All-Pro Fried Chicken franchises. I'm going to become the

Brady's wife, Anna, and her cousin await All-Pro's first customer.

first black franchisor in corporate history." He figured that 200 franchises meant a daily intake of $40,000. In a year the home office would gross at least $14 million.

Brady's mother-in-law, sharing his confidence, gave up her job to devote all her time to the expansion of All-Pro Fried Chicken. Her sons, James and Benjamin Brown, also joined the venture.

With great hopes, therefore, Brady opened a second store in San Diego. To his surprise, however, the second store was a failure. Analyzing the failure, Brady, admittedly unfamiliar with the eating-out habits of white suburbia, discovered that the store was poorly located. Adequate financing was needed for more attractive settings and better advertising.

Brady had learned a valuable lesson. He would have to have enough money "to take care of an occasional franchise problem." His only experience with having enough money was as a pro football star and soon All-Pro Fried Chicken would demand all of his time. Where, he wondered, was he going to get financing?

Until it was time to report to camp, Brady in past summers had worked for the Douglas Aircraft Corporation at Los Angeles, and now he was wondering whether he should work for Douglas again this summer.

Unfortunately, in Los Angeles he could find no men of his race who were familiar with the franchising world that Brady envisioned.

Initially, Brady had talked with Paul Lowe,

running back of the 1960–1968 San Diego Chargers, about investing $50,000 in All-Pro Fried Chicken. However, on the day they were to do business, Lowe could not give up his morning golf game; so Brady decided to give up on Lowe.

Brady's dream of a $500,000 loan as risk capital from white financers was a pipe dream for the rank and file of black men. The first problem was to find such men; the second was to persuade them to talk to a black man with no financial backing. Brady knew that the owners of the Steelers, the Rooneys, were very wealthy. Would they invest further in All-Pro Fried Chicken? A much larger investment would be needed for a nationwide chain.

When Brady reported for camp in July, the Steelers' organization gave Brady the use of office equipment he needed. And while a couple of Steeler veterans quit the camp, protesting Coach Bill Austin's torturous training methods, Brady's hope of working out a better contract made the camp conditions more tolerable for him.

At the same time that he was hoping for more money from football, Brady was looking for a Pittsburgh businessman with the contacts and ability to secure the needed financing for his business venture.

Meanwhile, he advertised his budding business by word of mouth at training camp. To impress both teammates and newsmen, he prepared and served them his All-Pro Fried Chicken. Some talked of buying interest in the corporation. Then he had the good fortune to meet Thomas Reich, a brilliant business attorney. He listened to the story of All-Pro Chicken with great interest. The fact that All-Pro Fried Chicken was taking on formal corporate shape and that there was talk of buying interest made Reich a very valuable business adviser.

Reich proved to be an expert in franchising matters, but he was not immediately sold on All-Pro Fried Chicken's being an independent operation. Having just purchased area rights to another fast-foods idea, "Mr. Sandwich," the attorney attempted to convince Brady that he should add his chicken delicacy to the several other varieties already planned for sale by the Mr. Sandwich franchise. "Brady Keys' Fried Chicken" could be developed as a part of the Mr. Sandwich corporation.

Brady resisted Tom's suggestion. He won Tom over to his side with a persuasive outline of the national possibilities of All-Pro Fried Chicken. The two men then agreed to make Brady the major corporate partner. Tom's share of the company would be 25% for the first year and 35% after that. At that time, except for the two stores in San Diego, All-Pro Chicken was mainly on paper.

Dividing his energies between pro football and business was wearing on Brady. He had begun to feel that he was being unfair to both the struggling Steelers and himself, but he convinced himself that playing his best during every game would take care of the Steelers. Nobody could dispute the fact that for the past two years, no touchdown passes had been completed in his area. It seemed that Brady's position on the Steelers was beyond challenge.

When the opening game of the season against the Chicago Bears arrived, Brady had a great afternoon and the Steelers won, 41–13. When the Steelers beat the Detroit Lions in their second game of the season, Brady relaxed a little. Then came successive losses to St. Louis, Cleveland, and the New York Giants. By the time of the loss to New York, Coach Austin's biting tongue was in furious motion. The coach insisted on changes in Brady's style. Deciding that the veteran player was lacking in several phases of forward pass defense, he insisted that Brady use techniques that had been perfected by Coach Vince Lombardi, the genius of Green Bay.

Instead of talking over problems alone with Brady, Austin began chewing him out in front of the whole squad, thus injuring the dignity of the six-year veteran. Clearly, a crisis was approaching.

Only about 26,000 fans showed up at Pitt Stadium for the game against the Dallas Cowboys. For 58 minutes, Pittsburgh rewarded their supporters with a forceful job and were leading, 21–17. It was second down and 7 to go at the Steeler 23. When the Steelers failed to gain first down, they punted.

The punt went out of bounds on the Cowboy 32-yard line. A forward pass was the obvious play. Before Don Meredith, the Dallas quarterback, could find a target, however, a Steeler pass rush nailed Ben McGee, 250-pound tight end with such force that he fell into Don, knocking him down for a loss of ten yards. From the Dallas 22, it was second down and 20 yards to go, with less than a minute remaining.

Brady had noticed that Lance Rentzel, wide-receiver of the Cowboys, had run a shallow down-and-out pattern on the last, aborted play. Anticipating the same maneuver on the next play, Brady told himself: "Here comes an easy touchdown, I'll break it wide open." Sure he had read Rentzel correctly, Brady was ready to pick the ball off the fingertips of the Cowboy star en route to the goal line.

Again Meredith was positioned for the snap. Brady took two cautious strides toward the out area —only to see Rentzel sprint past on an out-and-fly maneuver. Brady stopped, turned completely around, and pursued the Cowboy.

Meredith spiralled a 58-yard bomb into Lance's hands just beyond Brady's reach at the Steelers' 30. Jolted by Brady, Rentzel juggled the ball and lost control of it. Teammate Dan Reeves plucked it from the air and stormed 27 yards to the Steelers' 3. Seconds later, Dallas had a touchdown and a 24–21 victory.

Coach Austin walked off the field, his head down. The Steelers' dressing room was graveyard quiet. Newsmen gathered around Coach Austin, then rushed to the telephone. At 10 P.M. that Sunday night, the *Washington Post-Gazette* carried a front-page sports story. It was a four-column streamer: BRADY KEYS TRADED TO MINNESOTA VIKINGS!

6

Rising Franchisor

After six hours of restless sleep at a friend's apartment in the Shadyside section of Pittsburgh, Brady was awakened by an alarm clock. It was 7:30 A.M., Monday, 30 October 1967.

Awakening brought pain with it as Brady moved his badly swollen left knee. A routine injury at first, the knee got worse when Brady committed the "rookie mistake" of playing in exhibition games despite the injury. He forgot the basic rule of the "clubhouse lawyers": "When injured, never play in exhibition games, unless you're a rookie trying to make the team."

In order to play, Brady received painful cortisone shots before each game. Yet he never complained or even called Coach Austin's attention to the seriousness of the injury. All that the coach knew was that he was watching a different Brady. And while he admitted that he had guessed wrong on the play in the Dallas game, Brady's lame knee was an important factor in Rentzel's escape.

The thing Brady regretted most about leaving Pittsburgh was having to be away from All-Pro Fried Chicken operations at a critical hour. He would have to direct All-Pro by remote control from Bloomington, Minnesota, home of the Vikings.

At this point, Brady considered retiring from pro football and dramatizing his entry into business with a press conference announcing his retirement. However, he decided that his $40,000-a-year salary and the publicity value of being a football star were still valuable and needed assets.

While Brady was in Bloomington, Tom Reich would have to assume more responsibility for All-Pro Fried Chicken. Fortunately, Brady knew, Tom had the necessary qualifications to do a good job. So Brady and Tom went into a huddle that Monday and worked out the blueprints for their business future. They decided that Brady should fly back to Pittsburgh after every Viking game for conferences. The rest of the time they would talk by phone.

Thus Brady was able to report to the Vikings on Wednesday, 1 November 1967, with his mind at rest. Coach Bud Grant welcomed Brady, telling him how much improved Minnesota's chances were with a player of his ability on the team.

But the coach and Brady both knew that until his knee healed, Brady would not be able to play his usual game. So Grant made Brady back-up man behind Cornerback Ed Sharockman.

Brady was, however, instrumental in the Vikings' defeat of the Pittsburgh Steelers several weeks later. Not only did he play well against his former teammates, but Brady also helped Coach Grant devise the strategy for the game. Brady denied, however, that his fine performance was at all motivated by a desire for revenge against the Steelers.

During this time, Brady was working hard at learning the fast-food business and administering All-Pro Fried Chicken. Coach Grant did not like Brady's involvement with his business. He complained that Brady's preoccupation with money might distract the contented Vikings when they should be concentrating on football. Brady, on the other hand, felt that he was doing a good job for the Vikings.

Nonetheless, it was with a sense of relief that Brady saw the 1967 season come to an end, permitting him and Tom Reich to begin the difficult task of building All-Pro Fried Chicken into a national franchising business. Their first need was still sufficient venture capital. Where could a black pioneer and his Jewish partner find $500,000?

Within thirty days, Tom had sold their idea to Jack Kahn—a partner in Feldman and Kahn, an advertising and public relations firm. Kahn could not make $500,000 immediately available to the corporation, but he solicited support and interest from his friends.

At the same time, Mr. M. K. Mellott, the president of a Pittsburgh firm handling corporate mergers, acquisitions and financing, was struck by a newspaper report about Brady's plans for establishing a fast-food franchise business. Mr. Mellott talked to Brady and warned him about the difficulties of this type of business.

By that time, however, All-Pro Fried Chicken had established an administrative office in an attractive brick structure at 2945 Banksville Road in Pittsburgh, and was preparing to open its first franchised store at 3021 Banksville Road, just south of the office. The new outlet, fitted with poles from which NFL pennants and colors flared, was decorated inside with enlargements of football, basketball, and other sports heroes.

Represented by Feldman and Kahn, the new firm began shopping around for locations for more franchises. A two-year lease was placed on the home office. Plans were on the drawing board for ventures in such nearby Pennsylvania localities as McKeesport and Washington. Tom Reich proposed that three stores be erected in Syracuse, New York. Richard Metter, a wealthy Syracuse friend of Reich's, joined by John Hinerwadel, Jr., the son of a rich New Yorker, offered financial backing for the Syracuse stores.

These initial units in white areas served as the "launching pad" of All-Pro's program. They were

The first All-Pro franchise store opened in Pittsburgh in 1968.

experimental stores in many ways, opened primarily without any knowledge of site selection, lease negotiation, accounting controls, or training facilities. In short, they lacked most of the necessary ingredients of a successful franchised operation. When all three ventures in Syracuse failed, Brady realized that trained personnel was just as important as financing. Yet he was able to use those stores as leverage in other deals which were fundamental to the company's growth and development.

One by one, Brady and Tom faced the many problems of the franchising business. Tom was so engrossed in the problems that his law partner almost walked out on him. Tom and Brady became preoccupied with exhaustive studies of the dining habits of millions of people from suburbia to the ghetto.

For Brady, his ability to attract able white professionals to his business venture was a measure of his success. In the black American tradition in which he grew up, the hero was the man who successfully competed with whites. Jesse Owens, Joe Louis, Jim Brown and Willie Mays became sports heroes. Booker T. Washington and Martin Luther King, Jr., excelled in humanitarian endeavors. And Brady was determined that Brady Keys, Jr., was going to be an unprecedented success as a franchisor.

A major contribution toward that goal was made by Walter E. Gregg, the former president of Crucible Steel of Sharon, Pennsylvania. After a proxy fight,

Gregg left Crucible and in March 1968 joined All-Pro as chairman of the board. Brady attributed the completion of his corporate education to the instruction he received from Gregg, who advised him to make sure that all power was vested in him, the president. Brady never forgot those words.

Brady Keys, with his partner, Tom Reich (left) and Walter E. Gregg, chairman of the board of All-Pro.

7

A Visit to Wall Street

During the spring of 1968, Brady could almost taste success. Black people had had no history in multi-million-dollar industrialism. Now Brady and his associates hoped to prove that blacks could successfully enter the world of corporate billions.

Every morning, Brady climbed into his automobile and drove across Pittsburgh's complex of bridges, over the Monongahela River, and through the Fort Pitt Tunnel. He turned into Banksville Road and arrived at his home office, 2945 Banksville Road, to start his day at 9 A.M.

Brady, Gregg and Reich prepared profit projections for the next three to five years as well as a balance sheet of requisitions and justifications. They were convinced that they needed $3 million. They decided to go to Wall Street to get it.

By this time, Wall Street was reported buzzing about the prospects of fast-food franchising. Several brokerage firms had expressed a desire to confer with the representatives of All-Pro Chicken during their Wall Street visit. The fact that All-Pro was considering "going public" (offering its stock on the stock market) was a leading topic of interest. The Pittsburgh trio started out with five appointments scheduled for one day.

The great hour for the trio came. Smiles and handshakes greeted Reich, who led the way, and Gregg, who followed him. But it seemed to Brady that their hosts were taken aback by his presence. For a moment, he wondered if he should have allowed his two associates to handle the conferences by themselves. When no financial success resulted from the conferences, Brady was sure it was because he was black and the president and major stockholder of All-Pro Fried Chicken.

Despite that belief, Brady knew he had done the right thing in not withdrawing from the conferences. Brady was going to be the director of his own fate, even if it meant that All-Pro Chicken would fail from lack of financial nourishment by Wall Street.

Every Wall Street brokerage firm turned thumbs down on their proposition.

In July, with no prospects for financing having appeared since the Wall Street failure, Brady thought of Buddy Young, the ex-Illinois and NFL halfback superstar who was working on player relations in the New York office of NFL Commissioner Pete Rozelle. It occurred to Brady that Buddy might be able to put him in touch with some monetary sources.

Buddy was happy to see him, and listened to Brady explain that All-Pro Fried Chicken needed a financial angel.

When Brady had finished, Buddy told him that he knew somebody who knew somebody at the First National City Bank of New York. He went to make a telephone call. When he came back, he told Brady: "Tomorrow at 1:00 P.M., meet Ed Lewis at the First National City Bank."

Brady was ready to go at eight the next morning, five hours ahead of time. At one, when he arrived at the bank, Ed Lewis listened to Brady and then took him in to meet 23-year-old Edward Glassmeyer, an officer in the Capital Corporation department. Then Philip Smith, the young president of the Capital Corporation, entered the proceedings.

Brady felt encouraged. He was being given the chance to tell the All-Pro Chicken story to a good listener. The result was gratifying.

Glassmeyer told Brady that other bank officials would have to be briefed before he could act, since the possibility of considerable funding was involved. He told Brady to come back the next morning.

Brady stayed with friends that night, and he felt

Keys confers with officials of the First National City Bank of New York.

the way he had when he was preparing himself for the Pro Bowl.

When the three-hour deliberations came to an end the next day, Brady Keys had won the greatest victory of his lifetime. Glassmeyer outlined the terms of a business venture loan to this young franchising organization that included an immediate loan of $150,000. Within ten days, Tom and Brady had secured the $150,000 deal. At long last, it seemed that All-Pro Chicken was on the move.

8

Farewell to Football

Brady's success in providing All-Pro Chicken with its first substantial venture capital came at a good time. It was July and Brady once again had to report to training camp.

Ten months earlier, when Brady had left the Steelers to complete the 1967 season as a Minnesota Viking, Tom was left in charge of the firm. Now a $45,000 salary had lured Brady into signing a contract with the St. Louis Cardinals for his eighth NFL season, and once again Tom would be in charge of operations. As before, Brady could be in town only on Mondays; they would stay in touch by phone the rest of the week.

Remembering Brady's great defense as a Pitts-

In St. Louis, Brady became friends with another Cardinal—baseball star Lou Brock, who became an All-Pro area franchisor.

burgh Steeler against the Cardinals, Coach Charles Winner was happy to have him on his team. His knee injury healed, Brady was doing well in training camp. Then, rumors that he was a millionaire began circulating among the players, as well as accusations that he was too involved in his business to play well. In addition, that led at one point to a direct confrontation between a black and a white faction. That was the climate that existed on the St. Louis team when the Cardinals went to New Haven, Connecticut, for an exhibition game against the New York Giants in the Yale Bowl.

The team's mood was not improved when a crowd of New Yorkers that met them at the hotel was interested only in Brady.

Later, during the game, Brady held the hard-charging Homer Jones to one completed forward pass. He also intercepted a Fran Tarkenton pass, preventing a touchdown. He chased and nailed Halfback Ron Bly on what would have been a long, scoring run. Yet, for the first time in Brady's career none of his coaches congratulated him after the game. His reception by the sophisticated New Yorkers apparently was greatly resented. Usually sensitive to people's reactions, Brady had no idea that day that anyone had thought him offensive or out of line.

Things got worse after the season opened and the Cardinals lost three of their first four contests. During the fifth game of the year, Brady was at his very best, covering the great Paul Warfield with his usual defensive finesse and verbal assault. In a sensational play, Brady deflected the ball away from Warfield. As Brady was turning to follow his team off the field, he heard someone on the Cardinal's coaching staff shouting at him: "Hey, you idiot, why don't you run?"

Enraged, Brady dashed over to him. "Hey man, who're you talking to?" he demanded. Brady grabbed the fellow and threatened: "I'll kill you! I'll kill you!" A peacemaker intervened as Brady, trembling with rage, realized what had happened. He was immediately and permanently benched. His football career was over. Brady was sure that a malicious enemy, knowing how he would react, had arranged the whole incident to get rid of him. And he had fallen for it.

Brady had regrets. "I love football," he said, "and it's been good to me." However, he knew there was only one thing for him to do—return to Pittsburgh and work full time on All-Pro Chicken.

Thus, the great football career of Brady Keys, Jr., came to an end, as he dedicated himself to meeting and conquering another challenge: the business world.

When Brady returned to Pittsburgh, the first thing he requested was a complete report of what had been happening at the home office during his absence. He learned that Ed Glassmeyer had done a thorough evaluation of the All-Pro business. And Tom had carried on nobly.

Keys played his last season with the St. Louis Cardinals.

With other members of the All-Pro organization, Keys celebrates the opening of the first black franchise store in Brooklyn.

Tom believed that the federal government would lend an ear to any plan aimed at improving the ghetto and the lives of black citizens, and suggested that Washington, D.C., became an All-Pro objective. Shortly before he left Pittsburgh for training camp, Brady had received a call from Arthur McZier, who had just joined the Small Business Administration under Howard Samuels. While Brady went off to play football, All-Pro, under Tom's leadership, sought a way to establish its first inner-city franchise. It was decided to locate the store in New York City, in what they considered to be a potentially productive area. To operate it, Brady wanted a black man whom he could trust and work with. He chose Waldo B. Jeff, a friend from Colorado State College.

Waldo, with the help of the Small Business Administration, the New York Urban Coalition, and the First National City Bank, went into business with virtually no capital at all. The site in the Bedford-Stuyvesant area of Brooklyn was inconspicuous. The store opened in April 1969 and after three weeks of operation, was doing about $4,000 worth of business a week.

Mayor John Lindsay of New York samples All-Pro Chicken.

9

Capital and Conflict

Although All-Pro's future looked good in January 1969, when Brady left football, the company had used up almost all of the $150,000 received in August from First National City. Phil Smith of First National City arranged for Brady to talk with Bill Atterbury of the Ford Foundation. On February 23, the Ford Foundation invested $250,000 in the one-year-old firm. However, this was only interim financing until a deal could be worked out with one of Wall Street's oldest investment banking firms, Ladenburg, Thalmann and Company.

The firm's interest in All-Pro had been aroused by M. K. Mellott, an invaluable financial consultant to All-Pro. The brokerage firm dispatched a task

A billboard outside Pittsburgh spreads the word of All-Pro Chicken to travelers and residents alike.

force to Pittsburgh to evaluate All-Pro Chicken, and on July 23, with Mr. Mellott's help, All-Pro received a loan of $725,000 from Ladenburg, Thalmann.

As a result of the Ford Foundation and Ladenburg, Thalmann money, All-Pro Chicken had the working capital it needed. Brady, however, was not satisfied. He turned next to the Aetna Life and Casualty Company. In September, Aetna officials agreed to dispatch representatives to Pittsburgh for a first-hand inspection and evaluation of All-Pro Chicken. In October, Aetna, as the representative of the four firms that decided to participate (Travelers, Berkshire, and Connecticut Mutual), announced the investment of $2,200,000 in All-Pro Chicken. That deal made the total 1969 funding $3.3 million, although the Aetna official closing was not until April 1970. Aetna, Brady believed, had secured the firm's future.

Having thus won the battle for supporting capital for the moment, Brady concentrated his energies on a variety of test programs. With the capital for development projects, the firm would now find it possible to improve all of its productive equipment and methods. Efficient frying and a careful testing of batters and seasonings were planned as well as the writing of operating and accounting manuals geared to minorities.

All-Pro's future had never seemed brighter financially, and it was now time to consider reorganizing the structure of the company to meet the new challenges and demands of a growing business opera-

Keys talks over plans for a new franchise with former teammate, Lonnie Sanders.

tion. This need, however, set the stage for a policy struggle that would determine the future leadership of All-Pro Chicken.

For some time the once warm relationship between Brady and Tom Reich had been declining. Brady had been studying Tom ever since they had become business partners. As a result, Brady felt that he knew and understood Tom. "I guess Tom is one of the three smartest and most capable men I have come across in the formative years of All-Pro Chicken," Brady has recalled. He had observed how Tom worked with people; how he used words; how he was able to make a good impression with important people. But Tom and Brady had never completely resolved a serious disagreement over the question of accountability and many small disputes that had arisen during their association.

In late 1969, a major disagreement over All-Pro's administrative policies made Brady even more aware of the deterioration in their professional relationship. It was becoming clear to him that he and Reich could no longer work together in the company. Brady got in touch with Mr. Gregg, the chairman of the board, and suggested that a separate division of the company be created and that Tom be placed in control of it. That arrangement would have the added advantage of permitting Brady to observe how the other employees could function without Tom. Thus All-Pro Equities was established, as a temporary solution to allow everyone time to cool off.

10

The Presidency in Danger

This was the sad situation on New Year's Day, 1970. For the next two months All-Pro was in serious trouble, because the Aetna closing was not moving as rapidly as had been expected. Brady devoted his energies to improving the company's performance.

After considerable deliberation, he decided that the operating and technical services area was falling behind and becoming a detriment to the over-all progress of the company. An immediate solution, he decided, was for him to become involved in unit performance. After visiting an All-Pro Chicken unit in Harlem, which had been opened prematurely and was running poorly, Brady reluctantly took over unit performance from Phill Foster.

Tom, meanwhile, was extremely dissatisfied with the All-Pro Equities situation. Early in February, he began conferring with institutional investors in hopes of gaining their support in his effort to change administrative procedures and policies. On February 10 in New York, Tom discussed his approach to All-Pro Chicken with Edward Glassmeyer and Philip Smith at First National City Bank. But these two men had stood firmly behind Brady from the beginning, and Tom found them unsympathetic to his plans.

The following day, Brady received copies of two memos that disturbed him greatly. Both memos were from Arnold Gefsky, and the members of the board of directors had also received copies. Brady was concerned because they were executive memos that he had not dictated. He went directly to Arnold, reminding him that no official was permitted to take internal problems directly to board members.

Brady, however, finally realized that something important was wrong. So he took the memos home and read them over slowly six or seven times. Then, he called Ed Glassmeyer at home, because Arnie Gefsky's memo had reportedly been requested by Ed. Brady "cussed" Ed out for meddling with "my Pittsburgh personnel." Glassmeyer calmed him down and without telling Brady specifically what had been said, filled him in on Tom's visit the previous day. Brady did not sleep a wink that night.

He tried to recall all the things that had happened. He read the memos again and again. At 8:30 the next morning, he was at work.

Brady Keys showed strength and determination in maintaining his position as president of All-Pro Chicken.

First, Brady discussed the development with Mr. Gregg, his chairman of the board. Then he went to New York City, where he got the vote of confidence he needed from First National City Bank.

A board meeting was called for the end of the week on February 20. The intrigue and tension that week were great. Both Brady and Tom used the time to see where the employees stood. Ed Glassmeyer sent one of his confidants, Bill Riley, to mill around the home office and determine the attitudes of key executives. Glassmeyer himself decided to come to Pittsburgh a day early to look at the situation.

When the day of the board meeting finally arrived, Tom resigned as an officer of All-Pro Chicken. At the meeting the directors accepted his resignation, effective immediately. Reich agreed to stay on as a consultant.

By the end of the day, Brady had total responsibility for the company. All committees were disbanded and all decisions reserved to Brady Keys. The company was starting over again from scratch.

11

All-Pro Meets the Colonel

No sooner was he given total executive powers by the board than Brady delegated that responsibility to his vice-presidents, Phill Foster; Walt Thomas; and Reggie Smith. This left Brady free to devote himself to the future of the company and of franchising in general.

A month before the fateful board meeting, Brady had spoken before a U.S. Senate sub-committee on franchising. Franchising had received some adverse publicity during the previous months, and Brady attempted to point out the valuable possibilities of franchising both for the economy as a whole and for blacks. He used his own experience as an example of the opportunity franchising offered for black entrepreneurship.

Brady also detailed for the committee the exodus of the white retailer from black communities, and the need for a middle class that included merchants and businessmen within the inner-city communities. He noted that while white merchants who had been in business there for many years were defecting from the black communities, the vacuum they left was not being filled by black entrepreneurs. In fact, the majority of blacks left in those forgotten communities had neither the training nor the financial backing necessary to undertake any kind of project. One consequence of this situation was that many residents of black communities were having to travel over a mile to purchase staples. Franchising, Brady reiterated, presented a unique opportunity to change the economy of the ghetto because of the advantage for the black man seeking to own a business.

Brady's speech was an impressive analysis of the economy as he had personally experienced it.

Following the liberating events of the company shakeup, Brady was able to speak at a number of forums. Each time, he repeated his ideas. He called upon foundations and corporations to provide the financial backing first for special training programs and then for businesses for penniless but ambitious black entrepreneurs. His goal, he said, was the creation of a working organism of black and white Americans.

At the same time that he was making these public appearances, Brady was doing extensive research

NEWS FROM

Vol. I, No. 1 May-June, 1970

All-Pro Has A Bright New Look In Advertising and Packaging

Here's the new menu board as it looks in Willie Stargell's unit in the Ellis Hotel in Pittsburgh.

There's a bright new look to All-Pro Fried Chicken.

The cocky little bantam athlete, the company's first symbol, has hung up his helmet and retired.

In his place is a new logotype—a new symbol—a new menu—and new packaging.

The overall reason for the change is to communicate to our customers more clearly the fact that All-Pro is selling fried chicken, a delicious, juicy meal in a box that is the talk of everyone who's tasted it.

The new logo, which will appear on all our units, menus, stationery, advertising and packaging is centered around All-Pro Fried Chicken resting in a skillet.

Helpful Hints

Each issue, we will be featuring helpful tips from our unit managers. This issue's tip comes from Stan Harvey of Willie Stargell's Ellis Hotel unit.

Stan suggests that managers spend several hours a day working in the service area. This will give them an opportunity to meet and greet customers and see how their employes are performing.

Nine New Units Will Be Open By End Of Sept.

All-Pro is moving into the most productive six-month period in its history.

Nine new stores are projected to be in operation as part of our All-Pro franchise chain by the end of summer.

New stores scheduled for opening during the summer are:

Washington, D. C.—two units: 3931 Minnesota Ave., and the corner of 14th and W St.

New York—six units; Brooklyn — 526 Nostrand Ave. and Eastern Parkway at Pitkin Ave.; Queens—88-02 Sutphin Boulevard; Bronx—877 Prospect Ave. and 53 East 167th St.; and Manhattan—1933-35 Third Ave.

Kansas City—at 7503 Prospect Ave.

All units listed above are in existing buildings which necessitated major remodeling projects to bring them up to the high standards required by All-Pro.

Insurance Group Funds All-Pro With $2.2 Million

Brady Keys recently announced that All-Pro Fried Chicken has received $2.2 million in debt and equity financing.

Described as the largest institutional insurance package ever offered to a bi-racial business firm, the program was worked out with All-Pro by four national insurance companies.

According to Brady, the money will be used to finance the construction and operation of a number of new All-Pro units in inner city areas. Under terms of the agreement, All-Pro may repurchase its equity in the firm at the original cost of the stock plus 15% annual appreciation.

Insurance companies participating in the package include Aetna Life, Berkshire Life, Travelers and Connecticut Mutual.

John Moore, Aetna investment officer and spokesman for the insurance groups, noted that while risks may be greater in this type of financial involvement than in loans to established companies, the worthwhile profit potential certainly justifies the venture. He pointed out that the opportunity to provide substantial aid to inner city areas also influenced the transaction.

Newsletter Name Contest Underway

What about a name for this newsletter?

Come up with one, and you may be the winner of a $25 U. S. Savings Bond.

Starting with this issue, All-Pro will run a contest each issue and award a $25 Bond to the winner. The first contest in the series is to come up with a name for the newsletter.

Remember, it doesn't take special talent to come up with a good name. Just think of one or two words which best symbolize the idea of All-Pro Chicken, and you may be the winner.

In addition, we welcome any comments or suggestions you may have, either toward improving the newsletter or improving unit performance. We're getting the newsletter started, but once it's under way, it's your newsletter.

Send your newsletter name suggestions or comments to Linda Heglas, All-Pro Fried Chicken, 3021 Banksville Rd., Pittsburgh, Pa. 15216.

The deadline to qualify for the prize is May 15.

In the spring of 1970, All-Pro took on a new symbol for its advertising, and published its first company newsletter.

A franchise seminar at Boston College heard Keys speak of the advantages that franchising offered black businessmen.

on the Colonel Sanders' Kentucky Fried Chicken organization. KFC, as Brady referred to the firm, was doing $100 million worth of business a year. With 3,500 outlets in the world, KFC was the largest privately owned food purveyor in the United States. Only the armed services moved more food than KFC. Brady and his consultant, Mr. Mellott, had begun weighing different approaches to KFC as early as December 1969. By April 1970, Brady and Mellott concluded that KFC, under the administration of Kentucky-born John Y. Brown, Jr., was an excellent prospect for a joint venture with All-Pro.

Brady wanted to avoid being in the disadvantageous position of seeking out Brown. He preferred to have them meet as equals, each having something to offer the other. Therefore, as a trial balloon, Brady first had Mr. Mellott contact lower-level KFC officials. When everyone at that level had expressed interest, Brady made his second move.

Senator Williams, who had been favorably impressed by Brady's testimony before the sub-committee on franchising, was asked by Brady to contact Brown, urging a meeting between Brown and Brady. The Senator's assistant, Mike Roseberg, contacted Brown, and on April 21, Senator Williams wrote to Brown regarding Brown's invitation to meet with Brady on May 13. He informed him that Brady was eager to meet with him on that date. Thus, the conference between Brady Keys, Jr., president of All-Pro Chicken, and John Y. Brown, Jr., head of Kentucky Fried Chicken, was assured.

Brady flew down to Louisville, Kentucky, and was met at the airport by a KFC chauffeur. Brown was late for the meeting because he had been having lunch with Paul Hornung, the Notre Dame and Green Bay pro-football great. Hornung, a good friend of Brown's, had spoken highly of Brady during the meal.

"I heard some nice things about you, Brady," said Brown. "Paul says you come highly recommended. What can I do to help you?"

Brady set the tone for the rest of the meeting by saying: "I am not seeking help. You asked me here to see you, and I'm ready to listen. I'm the president of a company much like yours. A better question to ask would be: What can we do to help each other?"

The meeting was a success. Brown, who knew little about ghetto economics, had much to learn from Brady about ghetto life.

Brady returned to Pittsburgh with a tentative joint-venture agreement. Next KFC sent two men to Pittsburgh to research All-Pro Chicken. Brady decided against involving All-Pro with any of the other firms, such as Church's, Quaker Oats, the Mariott system, and the Playboy Clubs, that had shown interest in the company. In June, a final agreement on principle was arrived at with Kentucky Fried Chicken.

All-Pro joined forces with Kentucky Fried Chicken to form a third company, Brady Keys Kentucky Fried Chicken. Here Brady poses with Colonel Harland Sanders and Norman Haberman, vice president of KFC.

12

Investment in the Future

On September 15, at the Hotel Congressional in Washington, D.C., All-Pro's Brady Keys, Jr., and KFC's John Y. Brown formally announced their $2-million undertaking. The joint venture, in addition to being an advancement in the fortunes of Brady Keys, was a significant step toward blacks' beginning to benefit from their $33-billion-a-year purchasing power.

Better than any other young man of his generation, Brady was implementing what such pioneering black sociologists as W. E. B. DuBois advocated years ago. "Go into business," urged DuBois in 1905, "in order to develop the wealth and power needed to change the black man's position in American

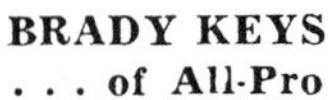

BRADY KEYS
. . . of All-Pro

COL. HARLAND SANDERS
. . . of Kentucky firm

Black, White Firms Form Partnership

By Aaron Latham
Washington Post Staff Writer

Two fried chicken companies, one founded by Col. Harland Sanders, who dresses like a Southern plantation owner, and the other started by Brady Keys, a black former pro football player, have formed a partnership.

The two companies announced here yesterday that they are forming a third chain that will operate in black

The formation of Brady Keys Kentucky Fried Chicken made the headlines.

Officials of Brady Keys Kentucky Fried Chicken with Mayor Walter Washington of Washington, D.C. (second from right), at press conference announcing All-Pro-KFC venture.

society." In 1970, sixty-five years later, fewer than 100,000 American blacks could claim ownership of a business venture. In addition, these 100,000 owned a limited variety of ventures. Beauty shops, barber shops, cosmetic manufacturing, and undertaking constituted over 90 per cent of such efforts. Only one black man has won the Spingarn Award* for achievement in business: the late Chicago banker Anthony Overton won acclaim two years before the Great Depression.

By these facts, we can measure the unusual accomplishment of Brady Keys, Jr., who, in his early thirties, convinced four firms to support his dream to the extent of $3.5 million, and who then entered into a $2-million partnership. President of the United States Richard Nixon recognized Brady Keys' unique position as one of the youngest and most unusual executives in the nation by appointing Brady to his national advisory council for minority business enterprise. Brady was also named to the President's Council for Carlow College in Pittsburgh, and made chairman of the equal-opportunity committee of the International Franchise Association. He became the first black to serve as a board member of that association.

In Pittsburgh, however, the site of All-Pro's home office, the financial community had contributed

* The Spingarn Award, presented annually since 1915, ". . . to the black man or woman who did most for the advancement of the race," honors the memory of Dr. Arthur B. Spingarn, a Columbia University professor, who, at the turn of the century, argued and won many cases for the NAACP.

nothing to Brady's dream. After he had completed the deal with Kentucky Fried Chicken, Brady knew he would have to devote himself to the problem of developing trained personnel. He decided to approach the rich families of Pittsburgh.

Brady was able to meet Henry Hillman, a member of one of Pittsburgh's richest families, and was invited to attend a ceremony honoring Hillman as top executive of the year in Pittsburgh. During his acceptance speech, Mr. Hillman told how he was trying to foster black entrepreneurship and spoke of what he was doing through the Allegheny Conference, an institution that lends seed funds to black men wishing to enter business.

Brady was surprised and impressed by Hillman's interest in black entrepreneurship. He approached Hillman after the speech and told him about All-Pro Chicken. Brady followed up this conversation with a letter, and, after some delay, a conference with Hillman was arranged.

After hearing him out, Hillman suggested that Brady call on two officials of the Pittsburgh National Bank. And with Hillman as a reference, Brady found a cordial reception where the year before he had been turned away. Not only did he get direct assistance from the Pittsburgh National Bank but Brady also got an introduction through the bank to Richard Scaife of the Mellon family.

After Brady had impressed Scaife with his plans for a nonprofit corporation to train blacks in business management, emphasizing franchising, the

Scaife family agreed in June to fund the Brady Keys Urban Talent Development, Inc., and appropriated $350,000 to train 2,000 blacks within the next two years.

After his successful encounter with the Scaife family, Brady found out from Mayor Peter Flaherty that he had goals in common with the city of Pittsburgh. The Model Cities program had money to provide for training in the Model Cities area, the same area that Brady hoped to serve with his training school. Brady's proposal that Model Cities money be directed into his school was favorably passed on.

It was through this fortuitous set of circumstances that All-Pro moved into another sphere of available financing—the government-funding area. Brady also asked the Mayor to allow him to develop the land at Crawford, Bedford, Webster and Wylie Avenues—a $20-million project. And he asked for funding for the Urban Talent Development, Inc., to experiment with a day-care center.

At this juncture, Brady went back to studying. He boned up on the Model Cities' program under HUD (Department of Housing and Urban Development), and on the Department of Labor and their funding programs. He also began studying housing, because he was convinced that the way to attain financial independence was through the ownership of real property.

Brady had come a long way. As a football player he had been driven by his uncontrolled emotions. While Brady retained his strong emotions, he learned to control them and subjugate them to his will to succeed. Starting out in San Diego in 1967 with a desire to make money, Brady grew with his company. He began to dream of greater opportunity for all blacks and with his characteristic determination convinced others to invest in his dream.

Now president of Brady Keys' Kentucky Fried Chicken as well as president and chief executive officer of All-Pro Enterprises, Inc., Brady has attempted to further through his own example the long-delayed goal of economic equality and brotherhood.

The ALL-PRO Creed

We believe that the arena, the stadium, the field revealing America at its best—are great teachers of honor, character and courage.

We believe that the rules of fair play and the stress of competition are great levelers that erode bigotry—and make it necessary to judge the performance, not the performer.

We believe that prejudice and its hateful brood of bigotry and intolerance wither and turn to dust in the heat of competitive sports.

Therefore, All-Pro Chicken, Inc., shall support these beliefs with something more than words by investing in the American dream.

We shall do this by contributing a percentage of our sales to this community—and to every community where we operate—to local organizations involved in sports activities for children of all races, creeds and colors.

Epilogue

by Brady Keys, Jr.

The extraordinary success of All-Pro Chicken has been possible largely because it is an "idea whose time has come." I believe in our country and in its economic system, but I feel that my people and I must be a part of this great system, because black enterprise must come to pass if our country is to continue to prosper.

The existence of small shops and manufacturing concerns is important to the plight of the black man, for reasons other than the income they bring in. Although the shopkeeper very often makes less money than the skilled worker, compared to the unskilled worker, who is often black, he has the possibility of achieving influence and perhaps great wealth. Furthermore, the small businessman gen-

Brady Keys with his wife, Anna, and his sons Brady, Rodney, and Jamie.

erally has access to that special world of credit which may give him, for a while, greater resources than a job. As he learns about finance, he develops skills that are valuable in our complex economy and capitalistic structure. He learns, too, about the world of local politics, and his knowledge may be valuable to a whole community or perhaps even to an entire race of people.

In spite of the advantages of owning a business, the black finds himself more underrepresented in business activity than in any other occapational category. More than 11% of the white population work as managers, officials, and proprietors, whereas the comparable figure for all non-whites is less than 3%. The percentage for blacks alone is even lower. The number of black-owned businesses is about 45,000 out of a total of some 5,000,000 businesses in the country. This fact has great economic significance in black communities. For example, in the important commercial activity of food retailing, no more than 3% of the black food bill is spent in black grocery stores. It also has psychological significance. Abraham S. Venable, Director of Office of Minority Business Enterprise in Washington, D.C., has said, "More often than not, many Negro businesses are symbols of frustration and hopelessness, rather than examples of achievement, success, and leadership. As a result, business per se is not a polite word in the Negro community, and Negro parents, as a rule, discourage their children from business careers, either as employees or as entrepreneurs."

Perhaps the most significant factor of all in the underrepresentation of blacks in the business world is the lack of managerial skills and attitudes. In the days of slavery, the plantation system offered blacks no experience with money, no incentive to save, no conception of time or progress—none of the basic experiences necessary to prepare them for a money economy. Thus, even today, blacks have had little exposure to business operations, and problems caused by limited managerial "savvy" have caused failure many times, even for an enterprising black who is competent in many aspects of his business.

With these factors as deterrents for the average black man, it's not hard to see that too often in the past successful black businessmen have preferred to adopt white middle-class standards, figuratively speaking. They have remained quite removed from the problems of the struggling black in the ghettos, and, as a result, have been unable to relate to them. All-Pro, to me is a response to this problem, and I feel it is the most important area where my company has succeeded. All-Pro has not remained aloof from the problems of the ghettoes, and has in fact been singled out as one of the leaders of the community.

Another area in which All-Pro's concept of national franchising has made great strides is its unusual approach to developing meaningful jobs for blacks on all levels. Simply decreasing the unemployment rate in the black community from 5% to 2% does not answer the black's need for self-determination and self-esteem. All-Pro believes that by creating several black enterpreneurs who are in the six-figure bracket in sales volume, and high five-figures in profit, one can do more to create, throughout the organization, the kind of jobs in which blacks can feel a sense of pride than by merely hiring a man or a woman to fill a position, as large companies and government agencies are attempting to do. It is my feeling that many companies have shown little initiative in the economic growth of the black man, because of their great emphasis on the importance of having a job.

"Black enterprise must come to pass if our country is to continue to prosper."

The key to All-Pro's approach to jobs, however, lies in the initial creation of black entrepreneurs. The experience of All-Pro in its corporate combination with KFC has shown that the future growth and development of the black entrepreneur can be successfully encouraged by cooperation between black and white companies. Another avenue that has not been fully explored is the spin-off arrangement, in which a large company creates a subsidiary, managed by blacks, and, after it becomes viable, "spins it off" as an independent business.

A relationship between a large white company and a struggling black outfit, or the spin-off of a black company, would bring respect not only for the two top executives, but for both companies, generally. The value of the counselling received by the black company would certainly result in the improved position of each business, but more importantly in the change in attitudes that each participant might experience from the relationship. It is essential, though, that both companies have a very sound organization. If this is lacking on the black side, the assistance will soon bear the stigma of paternalism, and if the white company has to give too much assistance, the benefits of the relationship may be lost forever.

I feel strongly that as more whites become exposed to enterprising blacks, and see that the twentieth-century version of the "plantation system" is not the way to go, they will learn that blacks are not generally lazy, but only without the basic business knowledge and acumen which is a large part of the white tradition. The one hope I have is that the many sacrifices of all of those who have given their best for All-Pro will improve the relationship between blacks and whites, to the extent that the dream of equality for all men will truly have been fulfilled.